OUR WORLD IN COLOUR

AJANTA & ELLORA

OUR WORLD IN COLOUR
AJANTA & ELLORA

Photography by Atul Kedar
Luca Invernizzi Tettoni, Photo Bank

Text by Ranjana Sengupta

The Guidebook Company Limited

Photography by **Fredrik Arvidsson** Front cover, 2-3, 5; **Atul Kedar** 16,
17, 18, 19, 20, 22-23, 28 (top), 31, 34, 35, 38, 39, 40, 41, 43, 45 (top), 46
(bottom), 47, 49, 50, 51, (top right and bottom), 52, 53, 55, 56, 57, 60
(left), 61, 62 (top), 64 (left top), 65, 67 (top), 72, 73, 74, 75, 76-77; **Luca
Invernizzi Tettoni** 6-7, 8-9, 12, 13, 21, 24-25, 26, 27, 28 (bottom), 29,
30, 32-33, 36, 37, 38, 39, 42, 44, 45 (bottom), 46 (top), 48, 51 (top left),
54, 58, 59, 60 (right), 62 (bottom), 63, 64 (middle right, bottom), 66, 67
(bottom), 68, 70, 71 (top), 78-79; **R Fotomedia Pvt Ltd.** 64 (left), 80;
Phillips Antiques, Bombay 10 (bottom), 11; **Toby Sinclair Collection**
10, 68-69, 70 (right), 71 (bottom).

Text and A-Z by Ranjana Sengupta
Captions and picture selection by Shobita Punja
Series Editor: Caroline Robertson
Designed by Au Yeung Chui Kwai
Artwork by Monica Tam
Created by Gulmohur Press

Printed in China

ISBN: 962-217-136-2

Cover
*Cave number 1 at Ajanta has
some of the best preserved
paintings, including the two
Bodhisattvas; Padmapani
and Avalokitesvara, shown
here.*

Title spread
*At Ajanta, 101 km (63 miles)
north of Aurangabad in
Maharashtra are a series of
twenty-nine Buddhist caves
excavated in the early
centuries of the Christian
era. The fine sculptures and
wall paintings within the
caves, behind the austere
façade, have been declared
a World Heritage Site by
UNESCO.*

Right
*Among the 29 excavated
caves, some are* chaityas
or prayer halls and others
viharas, *monastic living
quarters. The plan of the*
vihara *consists of a hall with
small cells, for the monks,
on either side. At the back
of the hall is a shrine with
a dramatic carved image of
the Buddha. The ceilings and
side walls are elaborately
painted.*

Pages 6-7
*The crescent-shaped gorge of
the Waghora River provided
an ideal setting for Buddhist
monks seeking a retreat. A
series of caves, monastic
dormitories and prayer halls
were carved into the hillside.
The caves seem to have been
abandoned for almost a
millennium before they were
accidently rediscovered in
1819 by a group of British
officers out hunting.*

Pages 8-9
*Ellora, 76 km (47 miles)
south-west of Ajanta, has
a group of Hindu, Buddhist
and Jain caves noted for
their sculpture. A few have
vestiges of painting. Cave
number 32, known as the
Indrasabha, dates from the
tenth century. The walls
of both storeys of the
Indrasabha have large
Jain images including the
Tirthankaras (Jain saints),
Gomatesvara, Parsvanatha,
Ambika and Indrani seated
on a lion.*

With the rediscovery of the Ellora caves in the early nineteenth century several British historians and artists visited them and have left us invaluable documentation of what they found. Capt. R. Elliott drew these pictures of the Buddhist *chaitya griha* (prayer halls) and *vihara* (monastic dormitory) in the 1840s.

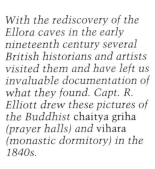

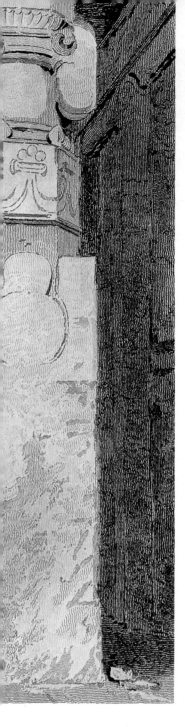

Nineteenth century aquatint engravings of the monolithic Hindu Kailash Temple and the Jain Indrasabha.

Left
The frieze at Ellora's Kailasa temple shows in miniature panels, scenes from the Ramayana and Mahabharata. Both stories tell the tale of heroic kings exiled from their kingdoms by scheming families and court politicians, their lives and trials in exile and final victories leading to the recovery of their rightful throne. In India, to this day, episodes from the epic poems are retold in theatre, dance, puppetry, sculpture and painting and are celebrated in national festivals.

Top
Cave number 30 at Ellora is popularly known as Chota Kailash, or 'little Kailash' as it is a smaller version of the magnificent temple number 16. This freestanding temple contains many carvings of Tirthankaras or Jain saints. The pillars of the shrine are often covered with dancing figures and floral designs, and there are a few remains of painting on the ceiling.

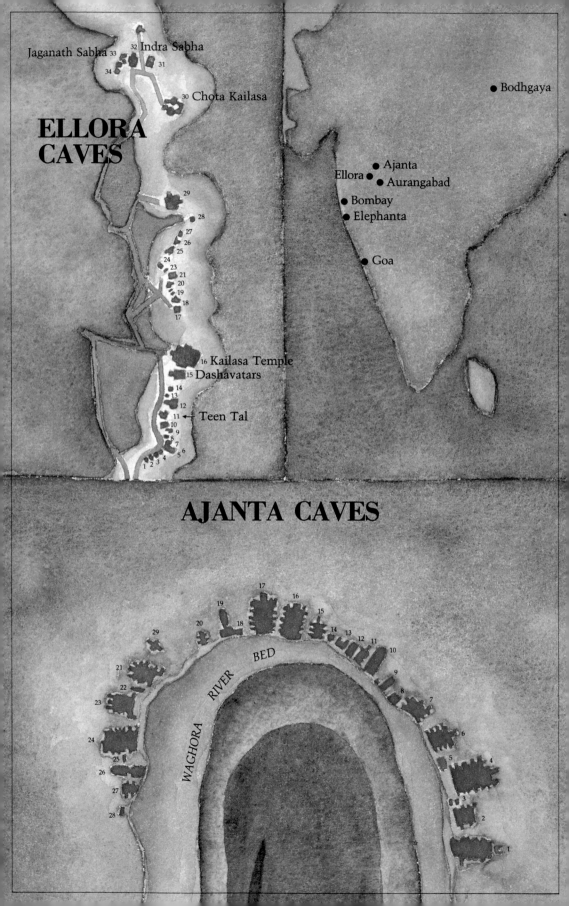

Jaganath Sabha 33   32 Indra Sabha

34   31

30 Chota Kailasa

ELLORA CAVES

29

28

27
26
25
24
23
21
20
19
18
17

16 Kailasa Temple
15 Dashavatars

14
13
12
11 ← Teen Tal
10
9
8
7
6
5
4
3
2
1

• Bodhgaya

• Ajanta
Ellora • Aurangabad
• Bombay
• Elephanta

• Goa

AJANTA CAVES

17
19
20 18 16
29 15
14 13 12 11
10
21 9
22 8
23 7
24
25 6
26 5 4
27 3
28 2
1

WAGHORA RIVER BED

INTRODUCTION

IN THE TWO CENTURIES preceding the birth of Christ, some exciting and innovative architectural experiments took place throughout Peninsular India. The finest examples of architecture from this period can be found in the Western Ghats inland from Bombay and in the Deccan area. Continuing until the tenth century AD, this form of rock-cut architecture, technically known as monumental sculpture, appeared at several sites in the region. The carving had to be mistake-proof; once cut it could not be replaced. At the beginning of the project an outline was made on the rock face, then the excavators moved in, working from the top downwards, so that the ceiling was completed first. Following closely behind, the painters, sculptors and finishers worked on each patch as it was cleared. The floor was reached by cutting long trenches downwards and the interspersed part of the rock—that not required for pillars—was knocked off. A painstaking process, achieved entirely with hand-held tools, the project was completed with an unquestioning faith in the value of the effort. Some caves did collapse, but most stayed upright, until over the centuries there evolved a whole series of rock-cut sites, the most significant and beautiful being those at Ajanta and Ellora.

Ajanta

The first wonder of Ajanta is the site itself. From a distance, in all seasons except the monsoon, the horseshoe-shaped hillside seems brown and barren. But those unknown men in the second century BC had taken pains to select this site. The curving gorge drops steeply to the Waghora River below. At one extreme, a waterfall drops through seven pools, or *satkund*. Idyllic, secluded and seemingly completely cut off from the world, this spot is an ideal location in which to search for the reasons for human suffering and answers to how they could be alleviated.

The caves follow the irregular outward curve of the hillside and are linked today by an uneven cement path. Earlier, however, individual caves were connected to the river by stone steps, almost none of which survive today. The gorge was a world in itself. The monks would get their water from the river and supplies from the nearby village. Intellectual stimulation came from Ajanta's situation not far from a trade route which linked the Arabian Sea to China. Travellers, traders and ascetics would come to seek wisdom at the caves and impart their own knowledge of the outside world. Thus the world of Ajanta was secluded but not isolated: an ideal place for contemplation. An inscription in cave 16 encapsulates the whole purpose of Ajanta:

'May this mountain, the peak of which contains various types of caves, which is inhabited by great people... and may the whole world also, getting rid of its manifold sins, enter that tranquil and noble state, free from sorrow and pain.'

The caves at Ajanta resulted from two distinct sets of historical circumstances separated by nearly five centuries. The earliest excavations date back to a period which covers the second century BC to the second century AD. The later phase of architectural activity, which came towards the middle of the fifth century AD, was one of the most spectacularly creative epochs in history. The architecture, paintings and sculpture that emerged and evolved in Ajanta at that time were to leave an impression on all subsequent Indian, Central Asian and Far Eastern art.

After the site at Ajanta was selected, finance was found from notables wishing to ensure their security in the next life (and perhaps some royal benefits in this one), artisans recruited and the first excavations inaugurated. Similar rock-cut architecture dating to this period can be found at several other places in the Deccan—at Bhaja, Kondane, Pitalkhora and Nasik, for instance.

At this time, more than a century had passed since the death of the great Emperor Ashoka, who had adopted Buddhism as a state religion. Buddhism had begun to lose its early momentum while Brahminism gradually took over. However, Buddhism continued to receive patronage in the north-western region as far east as Mathura, Sarnath, Orissa and in parts of western India.

A dynasty called the Satvahanas were ruling in the north-west Deccan during this early period. It says a great deal for the religious climate of ancient India, that despite their adherence to Brahminism, they encouraged and even patronised the caves at Ajanta. The caves of this period are relatively simple. During this, the Hinayana epoch of Buddhism, actual representation of human figures, particularly of the Great Teacher were absolutely forbidden; instead, geometrical

The facades of the caves at Ajanta, hewn out of the stark barren rock, form elegant porches and doorways with intricate carvings of Buddhist figures and symbols.

patterns and votive *stupas* were utilised to symbolise the religious truths of the Enlightened One. Six caves were excavated at Ajanta during this phase. Cave numbers 9 and 1O were the earliest, followed by numbers 8,12 and 13. While lacking the painted incandescence of the later phase, these caves undeniably have a stark grandeur that gives them great solemnity and dignity.

There were two basic cave designs at Ajanta, called *chaitya grihas* and *viharas*. Of the early phase, caves 9 and 1O are chaitya grihas. Chaitya grihas of the later phase can be seen in caves 19, 26 and 29. Chaitya grihas were halls of worship—large, rectangular chambers separated by rows of pillars into a central nave, surrounded by aisles on three sides, for circumambulation during prayer, with a sanctuary opposite the entrance. The sanctuary contained a votive image itself surrounded by an apsidal passage. The entrance would have a distinctive facade dominated by a large window evolved from the pipal leaf motif, which was to get larger and more elaborate as the centuries proceeded. The artisans of Ajanta attempted to recreate the feel of contemporary wooden architecture which was the model for the design of all of the caves. The high, vaulted ceiling was ribbed in a deliberate imitation of wooden beams. In fact, wooden beams were very often inserted into the stone roof. Similarly, the shape and ornamentation of the columns, window designs and doorways all imitate wooden and bamboo constructions.

The other basic design is that of the *viharas* or monasteries. These were rectangular-shaped halls with a series of small cells attached on two sides. The side opposite the entrance usually contained an image of Buddha or a votive stupa. Monks lived in these viharas, sleeping in the small cells that led off the main hall. The cells have stone platforms, perhaps used as beds, and were once separated from the vihara by wooden doors. Barring the five chaitya grihas, all the other caves at Ajanta are viharas, the best preserved examples being caves 1, 2, 16 and 17.

In the five hundred or so years that separated the first phase of excavation from the later, many of these painfully acquired techniques evolved and assumed a degree of tentativeness, an almost experimental quality. The later excavations were in the reign of the Vakataka ruler, Harisena (AD460—AD478). The Vakatakas were feudatories of the Imperial Guptas who ruled northern India and were also allied to them through a series of arranged marriages. Harisena's reign came during the long imperial sunset and this enabled him to considerably expand his domains. He was also a religious man, and while subscribing to Hindu beliefs himself, was more than willing to extend his patronage to the establishment of new caves at Ajanta.

Ever since 1819 there has been disagreement between experts as to the exact dates of Ajanta, or more specifically to the dates of the paintings. The basic controversy is whether or not the second phase of Ajanta extended to the sixth century. Recently, there seems to be some agreement that the real glory of Ajanta began to fade at the end of Harisena's reign, that is towards the end of the fifth century.

Ajanta's flowering was spectacular but brief and with the fall of the Vakatakas, the caves were virtually abandoned. Over the centuries, the painted princesses and carved kings watched bats take over and debris fill the sanctuaries. The caves were not totally forgotten: the locals always knew about them and over the years *sadhus* and other wanderers of space and spirit would seek refuge there. And so time passed until the caves were 'rediscovered' in a fittingly romantic fashion.

On 28 April, 1819, John Smith of the 28th Madras Cavalry was out boar hunting with some companions. While scanning the hillside for prey, he noticed the carved façade of a cave just visible from behind a tangle of shrubs and creepers. Curious, he and his companions scrambled up the hillside to take a closer look—and that is how the Ajanta caves became known to the contemporary world. The name of John Smith is known to us because he carved his name and regiment on a cave wall, a forgivable piece of graffiti under the circumstances.

The 'rediscovery' of Ajanta sparked off enormous interest and a spate of discussion and debate that continues to this day. While the architectural feat of Ajanta is staggering, and the carved stonework no less so, it is the paintings that have really captured the world's imagination. Today's visitors still marvel at their incandescent colours, their grace of composition and the drama of human life which they portray.

'The wall paintings at Ajanta,' said eminent art historian Stella Kramrisch, 'show the internal space of consciousness and its contents. They are a picture of the world receptacle, teeming with people, spirits and gods, their mansions, hermitages and pleasances...' The paintings essentially tell the stories of the *Jatakas*, the tales of the early incarnations of the Buddha, when he appeared on earth in the Bodhisattva manifestations. Some scenes, however, especially those on the cave ceilings, are from everyday life: men playing dice, a pink elephant in a lotus pond and a medallion filled with garlands and geese—a fascinating mixture of the magical and the mundane.

The paintings are clearly the work of a number of artists, but the overall effect is of one flowing, fluid whole. Preparing the wall for a painting was a meticulous, time-consuming affair: first a mixture of earth, sand, vegetable fibres, paddy husk and grass would be plastered on to the wall. Next a layer of mud, earth and rock-powder would be smoothed over and was allowed to dry. The binding medium was probably glue. Finally, a thin coat of limewash was added. The paintings were first outlined in cinnabar red, then an under-painting drawn before the final colours were applied. Many of the paintings were finished with a strengthing of the outlines and then burnished. The mineral colours were relatively few: red, yellow ochre, tetra verte, lime, kaolin, gypsum and for very, very special effects, lapis lazuli which came all the way from Afghanistan.

The artists painted from the mind's eye, 'the storehouse of the consciousness' as Kramrisch put it. Thus they were not sequential or proportionate, but each event flowed serenely into another, following a scheme of their own, past and future coexisting in the present. Thus the paintings follow their own internal logic and are true to their own time. And this may, perhaps, be the reason for their spontaneity and appeal today: the princess in the act of rising, the Buddha seconds after he has been tempted by Mara, the beggar glancing at the passing lady, wondering if a few coins are coming his way...

Perhaps the figure that most exemplifies this is the Bodhisattva Padmapani who dominates cave 1, through sheer grace rather than flamboyance. He exudes gentleness and a kind of divine innocence. Clearly a fastidious prince, he is depicted delicately holding the fragile blue lotus, his head bent sideways as if the weight of his ornate, jewelled crown is too heavy for his head. His half-closed eyes give him an air of meditation, almost of shyness, his cleverly painted limbs and torso look smooth and cool. To his left is the Bodhisattva Vajrapani. His narrow waist and the strings of pearls looped around his chest emphasise a steely strength in his limbs reinforced by the implacable determination in his face.

Caves 1, 2, 16 and 17 have the best preserved paintings and require days, not hours to appreciate. In cave 2, for instance, is the scene of Buddha's birth showing his mother, Maya, standing in the palace garden at Lumbini. Also in the same cave is the scene from

The Buddha in paintings and carvings is shown in a number of poses: seated, in meditation, teaching and reclining. A code of hand gestures were used by artists to indicate various episodes of the Buddha's life.

The interior walls of Ajanta were first excavated and given a plaster finish before painting commenced. The colours were prepared from locally available minerals such as yellow ochre, tetra verte, lime, gypsum, kaolin and lapis lazuli, from the Hindu Kush, which have retained their hue for centuries.

the *Mahajanaka Jataka*, where the queen and her attendants tempt the shipwrecked prince with all the arts of this world. The Prince is not moved, and the queen, a look of chagrin on her face, just cannot believe it. How can he withstand her oiled and coiled locks, her dhoti in the latest fashionable stripes and all the firm bosoms and sinewy waists of her sensuous attendants?

In cave 16 the royal presence of King Harisena is very evident. Says an inscription in this cave:

'He whose majesty was like that of Indra and Upendra, who by might of his arm, conquered the whole world, became the standard of the Vakataka race...'

Cave 16 contains some of the loveliest paintings at Ajanta: the conversion of Nanda and the Maha Ummagga Jataka, for instance. In the verandah outside cave 17 is the wondrous flying *apsara*, an ethereal figure in a black, bejewelled turban, the pearl tassels of whose necklace have been twisted by her heavenly flight. Her tentative smile and half-closed eyes hint at mysteries that no human will ever know. Across the entrance is the god Indra, narrow-waisted and graceful, his black locks flying under his pointed crown, greeting the Buddha on his visit to heaven. Fluffy clouds float gently in the background, two celestial nymphs (*gandharvas*) and one cherub are in attendance.

Inside cave 17 is the unforgettable scene from the *Vishvantara Jataka*. The dark prince is telling his wife that he has been banished. She sags against him with shock, her jewelled pendant dangling nervelessly from her hand, her plucked eyebrows arched in distress. Inside the wooden palace, attendants hover round the couple anxiously, carafes in hand. The floor has little white star-shaped flowers scattered on it... but you are left in little doubt that this royal lady's pretty and privileged life is inexorably coming to an end.

The paintings are so accurate in their portrayal of the sublime and the profane, that they not only give us a comprehensive picture of the times, but also bring home much of what is true today. The paintings are so overpowering that, perhaps inevitably, the sculptures get overshadowed. The sculptures and carvings are, in fact, equally remarkable and are some of the finest examples of their time. The columns, for instance, have rich and elaborate carvings and medallions and are embellished with scrollwork and richly carved capitals. Frequently (as in cave 1) *kinaras* and *apsaras* abut the central image in the shrine, in this case a seated Buddha.

Outside cave 19 is a particularly appealing piece of sculpture representing the Naga king and his consort. The Naga king is disposed comfortably on the rock seat with one knee bent. His wife, her hair in tightly bound braids, is rather squashed in the corner. Even the attendant *yakshi* lolls rather casually in the other corner, indolently holding a flywhisk.

Flying figures in Indian iconography do not have wings; rather their ability to fly is regarded as yet another of their divine gifts and their actual flight is suggested by their bent legs or the movement of their ornaments. The flying couple on the bracket of a pillar in cave 16, have their legs bent from the knee but otherwise appear to be floating effortlessly through the air. The lady is leaning an elbow on her consort's shoulders, almost as if her heavy headdress were throwing her off balance.

Cave 26 has some of the finest carvings of the whole cave complex. This cave was constructed under the patronage of a powerful monk, Buddhabhadra, and the artist and sculptures came up with some of their finest works here. The cave is dominated by the massive figure of the dying Buddha on the left of the entrance. He is lying on his side on a couch, flanked by two trees while a whole frieze of his disciples grieve below.

These are the wonders of Ajanta. In the days of its glory, hundreds of monks lived and prayed and pondered on the meaning of life and death here. This isolated gorge and the marvels it contains are a tribute to the piety, vision, creativity and sheer determination of the men who chiselled these wonderful caves out of unyielding rock fifteen hundred years ago.

Ellora

Ellora first appears to the visitor as an irregular ridge of rock rising vertically from the ground. Unlike Ajanta, access to Ellora is very easy, but like Ajanta its true splendour lies concealed within. The rock-cut architecture of Ellora can be divided into three groups and roughly three periods: Buddhist, Hindu and Jain. Ellora's charms are sometimes underappreciated because of Ajanta's fame; the visitor coming to Ellora after experiencing Ajanta's enchantments, is sometimes satiated with so much rock-cut architecture, but that is doing Ellora a great injustice, for here, in this outcrop of basalt rock is the culmination of this form. Ellora represents some three hundred years of great experiments carried out by different faiths with their very different iconography and structural compulsions.

The Buddhists first came to Ellora some time in the early seventh century AD and began excavating in the most accessible place, which was the southern tip of the rock face. Twelve such excavations were carried out between the seventh and ninth centuries under the early Chalukya and Rashtrakuta dynasties. The Hindu excavations overlap with the later part of the Buddhist phase, again bearing out the climate of tolerance and mutual respect for the other faiths of the time.

Five Jain excavations dating from the ninth and tenth centuries AD complete the phase of rock-cut architecture at Ellora. These were carried out under the patronage of the later Rashtrakuta rulers.

The Buddhist caves all belong to the Mahayana phase of the religion and contain some of the most impressive images of the Buddha. The first three caves, all dating to the seventh century are lofty, pillared halls with carved Buddha images fashioned on a large scale. Cave number 4, a *vihara*, is two–storeyed, but in rather poor condition today. The pillars here have rather interesting pot and foliage motifs.

The tenth cave in this group is known as the Vishvakarma cave because, some say, it was so beautifully fashioned that it came to be known after the artisan of the gods; others say it is called this because it is popularly believed to have been a great favourite of those belonging to the carpenter's caste. Whatever the legends behind its name, its fame rests on the fact that it is the last great chaitya hall to be carved in the Deccan. It has the impressive scale of the other monuments in the group including a particularly large hall surrounded by two storeys of galleries inside.

Cave 11 was known for a long time as *Do Tal* (two stories) to distinguish it from the next cave which was called *Teen Tal* (three stories). But it was subsequently discovered that Do Tal was in fact Teen Tal and that the basement had been buried by several centuries of earth. The adjacent Teen Tal has a rather impressive starkness, a little spoilt today by the fact that the frontage, which was crumbling, has been repaired with enormous slabs of concrete. This huge vihara once had enough cells to house over 40 monks, today it echoes rather emptily to the footsteps of visitors and the flight of bats.

These excavations were carried out at a time when the impetus of Mahayana

The ceilings of the caves were carved and often painted with geometric designs, while walls and pillars carried narrative sculpture and murals pertaining to the life of the Buddha.

Sculptured images in the caves at Ellora are of Hindu, Jain and Buddhist deities and their consorts, auspicious symbols of apsaras, *tree nymphs, attendants of the gods, animal motifs, trees and plants.*

Buddhism was already declining; Buddhist excavations at Ellora had, in fact, virtually ceased by the close of the eighth century. Hindu excavations had already begun the previous century, the first of the 16 excavations having started in the early decades of the seventh century. The 16 excavations in this group extend along the west face of the hill for about a mile, the early seventh century *Ravana ki khai* being the first in this series. The plan of this excavation is simple, belonging to an earlier time—a smallish single hall with an image of the goddess Durga, now broken. Other carvings, however, of the goddess Laksmi, of Parvati and the god Siva, survive intact.

The Rashtrakuta king, Dantidurga, gave a donation for cave 15 when work was in progress in the mid-eighth century. This cave, known as the Dashavatars (ten incarnations) was begun as a Buddhist monastery though it was later excavated as a temple. The Hindus adopted the earlier Buddhist cave design and plans, adapting them to their own needs. A richly carved *mandapa* stands in the open court and the figures on the friezes are those that are repeated throughout the temples of this group—such as Siva and Parvati playing dice, their marriage and their disturbance by Ravana.

The ultimate culmination of rock-cut architecture, in terms of sheer mastery of technique and dazzling conception, is cave 16, better known as the Kailasa temple. Kailasa, perhaps fittingly, refers to the god Siva's abode in the mountains and was excavated under the patronage of the Rashtrakuta ruler Krishna I, who ascended the throne in the mid–eighth century. Work on the temple continued under his descendants for a hundred years.

Kailasa is a temple, conceived as a mountain, some three stories high, carried by a frieze of huge elephants. The temple itself is richly carved and embossed, the whole being an amazing example of the imagination, engineering skill, labour and perseverance of those who brought it into being. The making of Kailasa involved the cutting of three huge trenches at right angles from the top of the hill downwards, the three excavated areas forming the open court around the temple. The standing mass of rock in the centre was eventually hewn into the exquisite proportions of the temple itself. The hillside is about 30 m (100 ft) high and one can only speculate as to the time this massive task must have taken. One estimate is that roughly three million cubic metres of rock had to be excavated to make Kailasa possible. As in Ajanta, work proceeded downwards, the sculptors and carvers working on the top storey as the other masons continued to excavate the trenches.

Kailasa is approached by an archway, the topmost storey of which is connected by a bridge to the temple complex. A Nandi shrine opposite the entrance is flanked by two 15 m (51 ft) columns *(dhwajasthambas)* which are flanked in turn by two elephants. The temple itself rests on a very high plinth and contains some of the loveliest carvings in the whole hillside, including exquisite portrayals of Siva, Parvati, Nataraja as well as scenes from the *Ramayana* and the *Mahabharata*. The sanctuary is entered through an ornate doorway flanked by images of various river goddesses.

The cloisters ring all three sides of the courtyard with the Lankeshwara shrine situated towards the northern end. At the courtyard level there is a shrine to the three river goddesses—Saraswati, Ganga and Jamuna. Opposite this, across the courtyard, is the hall of sacrifice. Throughout the cloisters ringing the courtyard are sculptural friezes, mainly of the gods Siva and Vishnu.

Kailasa, it is said, resembles the earlier Virupaksha temple at Pattadakal which was associated with the coronation of the early Chalukya rulers. While there are certainly some similarities, Kailasa is unique. Art historian Percy Brown has called Kailasa 'the most stupendous single work of art ever executed in India'. While others may disagree, it is undoubtedly the apogee of all rock-cut architecture in India.

Of the remaining caves in the Hindu series, cave 21, known as Rameshwara must be singled out for its beautiful sculptures.The goddesses Ganga, Jamuna and Parvati, and the gods Siva and Kartikeya all figure on the friezes. Cave 29, Dhumar Lena, is said to be influenced by the pattern of the caves at Elephanta near Bombay. It is certainly amongst the most imposing on the site and dates to the late sixth century. The Ganesha Lena and the Jogesvari groups were excavated over two hundred years later, in the ninth century and are basically a series of shrines located high on the hillside. They were the last Hindu excavations to be completed at Ellora.

The Jain group of caves on the northern projection of the hill are set a little apart from the others and were begun around AD 880. There are five caves in all, but of these only three are considered to be significant. All three display to perfection the richly carved details and the polished finish which is the hallmark of Jain art. Cave 30 is known as Chota Kailasa for rather obvious reasons. It is a rather stunted copy of cave 16 but about a quarter of the original size. Inside are images of the Tirthankaras and of Mahavira Jain on his Lion throne.

Cave 32, the Indra Sabha, is so richly carved and decorated that it occasionally becomes rather overwhelming. The sides of the temple are covered with elaborate carvings of elephants, lions and vases. If you look closely at the roof you will see traces of maroon and green paint, leading one to speculate that in its prime the temple must have been very elaborately ornamented.

Early in 1990 some caves belonging to the Hindu series were 'rediscovered' at Ellora by staff of the Archaeological Survey of India, rather in the way that John Smith 'rediscovered' Ajanta. The caves are on the north-eastern side of the ridge and are mainly dedicated to Mahesha, an incarnation of Siva. Buried under centuries of rock and debris, some are still to be cleared. There are other subsidiary caves near Ellora which are yet to be opened to public viewing.

With the completion of the last of the Jain temples in the early part of the tenth century, work at Ellora, which had been continuing for well over three hundred years, was finally completed. Yet the pinnacle of achievement had been reached a long time before this with the remarkable Kailasa temple. Kailasa represented a break from the early traditions of rock-cut architecture, when the convention had been to work inwards. Kailasa was a rock-cut monolith, hewn in one piece from living rock. Temples ceased to be dark, pillared caverns and became open to the sunlight. Thus with Ellora the age of rock-cut architecture reached its climax and its end. But the achievements on that single piece of hillside are a lasting tribute to the imagination and faith of those who made them.

The walls of many of the caves depict well-known legends and myths of the gods. The darkness within and the monumental size of the images creates an atmosphere of mystery and awe. A fabulous larger-than-life sized Nataraja, reveals the scene of the Cosmic Dance of Siva, accompanied by musicians and celestial onlookers.

Following pages
In accordance with Buddhist principles human beings should lead a life sympathetic with nature. Establishing places of retreat in remote hillsides is an ancient practice in India, continued today by Hindu ascetics living in the Himalayas. Natural caves led to larger man-made excavated ones throughout the subcontinent. The best of those surviving are at Ajanta and Ellora.

Previous pages and right
A court scene in cave number 1, possibly the story of the conversion of Nanda. This is often repeated in Buddhist iconography because of its haunting theme. Nanda, a fellow prince like the Buddha, decided to join the Buddha's monastic order. His dilemma was leaving his wife Sundari (literally 'the beautiful one') and the pleasures of princely life for one of austerity, sacrifice and discipline.

Opposite page
Buddhist icons were sculpted according to a set of codified rules that used symbolic hand gestures and motifs such as the wheel, the deer, the throne and the sacred Bodhi tree. Each represents a stage of the Buddha's life. This figure of the seated Buddha in the pose that depicts the teaching of the principles of the Middle Path is in the inner shrine of cave number 2.

Research into the techniques of Ajanta mural painting has shown that the artist started with an outline of black or brown, before filling in the details of figures, clothing and jewellery with highlights in painted relief. Figures were painted in different shades or even different colours, to stand out by contrast with each other. The eyes of the religious figures are portrayed as though half closed in meditation with eyebrows poetically described as being 'curved like bows'.

Opposite page
Detail of the Bodhisattva Padmapani in cave number 1, holding a lotus.

It is in the female figures in the paintings of Ajanta that one sees the true mastery of the artist. In cave number 1 a magnificent array of colours, hairstyles, poses and costumes can be seen. In this painting (above and right) a woman leans against the wooden pillar of a mandap, or hall, and looks on at a group of female musicians accompanying a dancer.

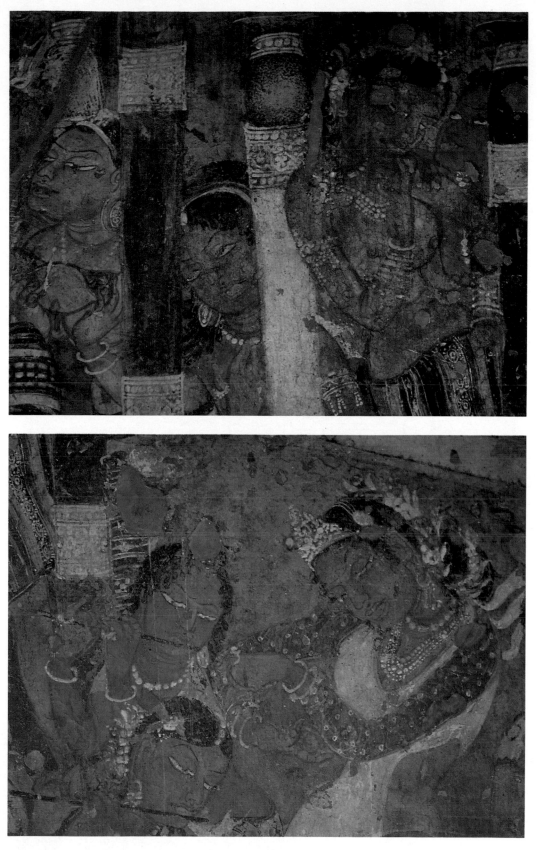

Following pages
In cave number 2, on the side walls leading to the shrine is a series of seated Buddhas with varying hand gestures to depict the scene of the Miracle of the Buddhas.

The lotus is used by the artists of Ajanta as a symbol of purity and goodness. Lotuses grow in still waters, from which they rise, clean and pure. A spray of lotuses with buds and full blooms also represents the eternal cycle of birth, life and death.

Opposite page
To excavate the caves at Ajanta the architects had to have a detailed and precise concept of their work in rock-cut architecture, as any mistake could not be corrected by rebuilding. In Ajanta, we see the architect-artists' phenomenal knowledge of geology, mathematics and rock carving. The patient chiselling of the rock to create the caves is a testament to their faith and dedication.

Above
*The ogress Hariti and her consort Kubera in Ajanta's cave number 2.
Hariti devoured little children until the Buddha hid her favourite
child. She then realised the agony of mothers who had lost their
children, and reformed.*

Right
*Cave number 2, one of the better preserved monasteries with a
shrine, shows how sculpture, painting and architectural elements
were used together to enhance the atmosphere of piety and sanctity.*

Taking their inspiration from contemporary architecture, the artists strove to reproduce in stone, beams, pillars, lattice screens, railings and the very shape of the arched windows—such features as would have been used in wooden buildings. The chaitya, or prayer hall, of cave number 9 is believed to be one of the earliest at Ajanta.

Left and far left
In cave number 7, a sculptured frieze of the miracle of Sravasti, when the Buddha multiplied himself a thousand times.

There are several chaitya grihas *or prayer halls at Ajanta. The plan consists of a central nave with pillars, behind which is a circumambulatory passage. The hall is often apsidal in plan or with a curved back wall, possibly taken from a wooden design. Within the curved end a stone miniature* stupa, *or emblem of the Buddha, was carved to serve as the focal point of the prayer hall.*

The paintings at Ajanta depict stories from the Jatakas or tales of the previous incarnations of the Buddha. In this scene, from cave number 17, a Raja is seen giving alms. The act of giving, of sacrifice and generosity is a theme often repeated in the Jatakas as parables.

In cave 16 the combined media of painting and sculpture adorn the dark interiors. These caves must once have been lit by oil lamps that cast a warm flickering glow onto the walls, bringing the images to life.

Above the doorway in the verandah of cave 17, is a row of amorous couples above which is a row of seated Buddhas. The raised right hand, with the palm facing the viewer, is a symbol of abhaya, *reassurance and protection.*

The Buddha is shown seated in padmasana, or the lotus pose of meditation. He is often shown with his hair tied in a top knot surrounded by a halo of light, representing nirvana *or enlightenment.*

48

Cave number 17. At one end of the verandah is a scene identified by scholars as the scene from the Vishvantara Jataka, of a prince who gave away his belongings in alms. This scene provides interesting information of contemporary wooden architecture, costumes and a glimpse of courtly life.

49

Cave 19 at Ajanta is amongst the best surviving examples of a rock cut chaitya griha. The elegant porch is topped by the distinctive 'horseshoe' shaped window, which is flanked by yakshas or guardians, standing Buddha figures and elaborate decorative motifs.

The interior of cave 19 is profusely carved with pillars, a monolithic carved symbolic stupa and images of the Buddha which heralded the introduction of the Mahayana phase. The story of Buddha's life served as a perfect example of his philosophy of compassion. Born as a prince, young Siddhartha renounced his wealth and position to find the meaning of life.

Seated under a Bodhi tree at Bodhgaya, the Buddha meditated, during which he was tempted by Mara and her voluptuous daughters. Lowering his hand, Buddha touched the earth to witness his enlightenment. The **Parinirvana** (ultimate enlightenment or liberation) came when Buddha left the world—as depicted in the 7m (23ft) image of the reclining Buddha in cave number 26.

Pages 56 and 57
Ajanta provides a unique opportunity to study the early phases of Buddhist sculpture, painting and architecture which later influenced artistic traditions in central Asia and the Far East.

Left and above
The Kailasa temple at Ellora, one of India's greatest architectural treasures, was hewn out of the solid rock of the hillside to form a free-standing temple consisting of a gateway, two-storied halls and the main shrine within. Unlike traditional architecture which is built up from its foundation, this temple has been carved downwards. While it adheres to architectural principles with pillars, roofs, windows, doorways and beams, it is in fact a monumental sculpture.

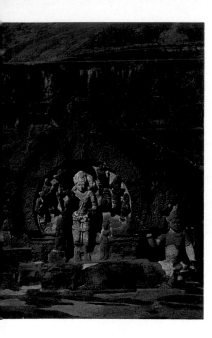

The scale of this sculpture can be gauged in relation to the human figures (far right). The architectural design of the Kailasa temple derives its inspiration from southern India. The shikara, or main temple tower, consists of a pyramid made up of well-defined horizontal diminishing tiers crowned by an eight-sided cupola. The pyramid represents the symbolic mountain abode of Lord Siva, Mount Kailasa. The different levels are peopled with figures of minor deities, attendants and guardians of the directions.

One of the most beautiful elements in the caves at Ellora is the variety of carved pillars. The columns are all sturdy and have massive proportions to suit the size and scale of the caves in which they belong. Some pillars are plain, others have carved bases, capitals, brackets and fluted shafts.

At the Kailasa temple there is a magnificent representation of Mahishasuramardini: *the killing of the* asura *(demon) named Mahisha. In this episode the gods pool their strength to create a 'super goddess', shown riding on her lion vehicle, to destroy the demon, Mahisha, who appears in this panel with the horns of a bull, while the gods are shown above watching this dramatic episode.*

Left
Tripurantaka. The three cities of the world (Tri-pura) in Heaven, Sky and the Earth were occupied by evil forces. Siva rides on his chariot, with Brahma as his charioteer, and, with the accumulated power of the gods, destroys the three cities with a single arrow. The panel shows a youthful Siva with his bow-string taut, ready to release his arrow and restore peace to the world.

Top
In another episode Siva, having destroyed the demon elephant dances in triumph with the skin of the creature.

Within the courtyard of the Kailasa temple are free-standing pillars and monolithic elephants. The side walls of the surrounding hillside have also been excavated to form halls. The walls of the main temple illustrate episodes from the Puranas *and epics, punctuated by figures of flying celestial couples.*

Rock-cut architecture or, more correctly, monumental sculpture, is found along the west coast of India, around Bombay, Karli and Kankeri; at Mahabalipuram near Madras in South India; Badami in northern Karnataka; and Udaigiri in Orissa. Monumental sculpture is also found in Ethiopia, Egypt, Afghanistan and China.

The three-tiered cave number 12, known as Teen Tal, is a
Buddhist chaitya or prayer hall and vihara, or monastery.
The impressive façade is unadorned, while the halls within
are decorated with a wealth of sculpture, of figures of the
Buddha and Bodhisattvas (potential Buddhas who renounce
Nirvana to preach for the benefit of humanity and guide
mankind towards the path of non-violence).

Capt. R. Elliott of the Royal Navy sketched cave number 10 in the early 1840s, and a popular series of engravings were made from his works. The chaitya hall had a decorative façade with a small horse-shoe shaped window. This window design loses its dramatic size when compared to earlier chaitya hall windows at Ajanta. In the course of evolution the window at Ellora has been reduced to a mere motif.

Within cave number 10 at Ellora, at the far end of the chaitya hall, is the main image of a seated Buddha (right) with attendants in front of a sculptured stupa. In the early Hinayana shrines at Ajanta the Buddha's image was not shown. Here the transitory phase is seen where images of the stupa are combined with figures of the Buddha in the Mahayana phase.

In cave number 21, called the Ramesvara Cave, the façade of the hall (opposite page) consists of a low parapet wall with images, above which are squat pillars with bracket figures representing the goddesses of the holy rivers of India. Foremost among them is Ganga, personified as a woman, as shown in this nineteenth century print (below), while the Goddess Sarasvati, of learning and music, is guardian of the southern direction, and also personifies a mythical river in northern India (left).

Unfinished caves and pillars provide a fascinating insight into how the artisans worked. Each part was fashioned, polished and completed in stages.

It was customary to embellish all parts of the religious structure with sacred motifs. The Kailasa temple (left) is shown as if carried by huge elephant caryatids (top left); similar elephants and lions are found on the balcony and parapet walls.

Top right
A superb example of Indian narrative style and composition. The story of Vishnu's incarnation as Narasimha is often depicted at Ellora. A demon king was granted a boon that he could not be destroyed by day or night, by man or beast, within the house or without. Vishnu in the form of half-man/half-lion is shown attacking the demon at dusk at the threshold of a house, thereby overcoming the limits of the demon's protection.

Following pages
Cave number 21, or Ramesvara.

Pages 78–80
Looking at the arid countryside around Ellora one can only admire the imagination of the original architects for creating such marvellous beauty from such a barren landscape. The fruit of their imagination remains as one of India's gifts to the world.